BUILDING

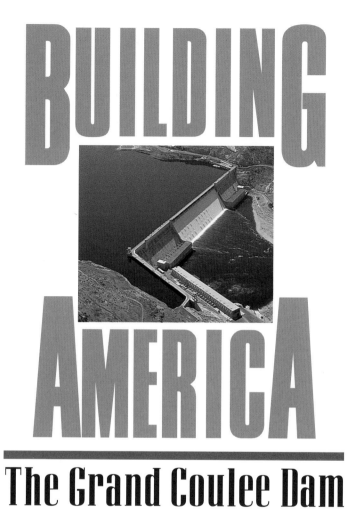

AMERICA

The Grand Coulee Dam

Marcia S. Gresko

A BLACKBIRCH PRESS BOOK

WOODBRIDGE, CONNECTICUT

Author's Dedication

To my most avid readers—Jessica and Joe

Special Thanks

The publisher would like to thank Grand Coulee historian, Wm. Joe Simonds, MA, of the Bureau of Reclamation for his help in reviewing the material in this book.

Published by Blackbirch Press, Inc.
260 Amity Road
Woodbridge, CT 06525
web site: http://www.blackbirch.com
e-mail: staff@blackbirch.com

© 1999 Blackbirch Press, Inc.
First Edition

Printed in Hong Kong

10 9 8 7 6 5 4 3 2 1

Photo Credits

Cover & title page: ©Craig Sprankle/Grand Coulee Dam; pages 4, 7, 41: ©PhotoDisc; pages 8, 14: ©Steve Terrill/Oregon Tourism; page 11: courtesy Library of Congress; page 17: courtesy Herbert Hoover Presidential Library; page 18: (top) courtesy Franklin Delano Roosevelt Library, (bottom) courtesy National Archives; page 19: (top) courtesy Bureau of Reclamation, (bottom) ©Corel Corporation; pages 20, 22, 25, 26, 28-30, 32, 38, 40: courtesy Bureau of Reclamation; page 34: courtesy National Archives; page 36: courtesy National Park Service/Harry S. Truman Library; page 42: courtesy Grand Coulee Dam.

Library of Congress Cataloging-in-Publication Data

Gresko, Marcia S.
   Grand Coulee Dam / Marcia S. Gresko.
        p. cm.—(Building America)
   Includes bibliographical references and index.
   ISBN 1-56711-174-2
    1. Grand Coulee Dam (Wash.)—Design and construction—Juvenile literature. 2. Grand Coulee Dam (Wash.)—History—Juvenile literature. I. Title. II. Series.
TC557.G64 G74   1999   98–46855
627'.82'0979731—dc21   CIP
                                           AC

Table of Contents

Introduction

Fed by snow and great ice fields in the Canadian mountains, the Columbia River begins in Columbia Lake in southeastern British Columbia. It is the fourth-largest river in North America—1,243 miles long. Into it flow the brooks, streams, and rivers in an area of more than 250,000 square miles, much of the Pacific Northwest. The powerful Columbia carries water from Canada and parts of seven states: Washington, Oregon, Idaho, Montana, Wyoming, Utah, and Nevada.

As the raging river surges from its source to the sea, it falls 2,600 feet. Its rapid rush makes the river the greatest source for water power in the world. More than 50 dams have been built on the mighty Columbia, harnessing its tremendous power.

Opposite:
Workers stand on top of some of the massive pipes that make up the Grand Coulee Complex.

5

Grand Coulee Dam straddles the river 90 miles northwest of Spokane, Washington, near the head of the Grand Coulee, a steep-walled canyon where the river once flowed. Although the giant dam was first planned as a way to bring water to the surrounding desert area, it is the greatest single source of hydroelectric power in the United States and the third-largest in the world. Its 3 powerhouses generate between 19 and 20 billion kilowatt hours of electricity per year—more power than a million locomotives could produce! The value of the electricity the dam generates each year is more than $462 million.

Hailed as one of the seven modern engineering wonders of the United States and the "eighth wonder of the world," Grand Coulee Dam was the largest dam ever built when it was completed in 1941. It stands 550 feet high—as tall as a 46-story building. It is 500 feet thick at its base. A special maintenance submarine checks its condition below the surface of the water. The top of the dam is nearly a mile long. The total weight of the structure is more than 22 million tons. It contains almost 12 million cubic feet of concrete—enough concrete to build a 6-foot-wide sidewalk around the world at the equator!

More than 12,000 people worked to build Grand Coulee Dam, and at least 72 men died doing it. Nearly a dozen new towns were created in the area to provide housing and services. Estimates report that 150 million hours of human labor went into the dam's construction—including work in the mines and factories, which filled more than 50,000 railroad cars with the materials needed.

Begun in 1933, Grand Coulee Dam took more than eight years to build. The original dreams and schemes for harnessing and using the power of the Columbia River began at the turn of the century with the first settlers in the area. By 1941, after battling a host of conflicting political agendas and money shortages, the "greatest structure on earth" was finally completed.

The turbines in the Grand Coulee's three powerhouses generate more electricity than a million locomotives could produce.

1

"Wheat, Heat, and Rattlesnakes"

An 1882 government survey of the land around the Columbia River described it as a dry, lifeless desert. But it hadn't always been that way. About 30 million years ago the area was covered by an enormous inland sea—the ancestor of the Columbia River. Then, 10 to 20 million years ago, violent volcanic eruptions spread waves of lava across the land creating the Columbia lava plateau and shaping the course of the river. During the Ice Age that followed, two important events occurred that formed the Grand Coulee. First, between 1 and 2 million years ago, a glacier blocked the Columbia River and forced it into digging a new, temporary channel. Second,

Opposite:
The rugged landscape of the Columbia River basin provided a challenging environment in which to build the world's largest dam.

9

the greatest floods in Earth's history repeatedly swept down from an ancient glacial lake. Approximately 20 miles wide, more than 600 feet high, and moving at speeds of almost 50 miles an hour, these raging floods carved a new canyon, or coulee. The coulee, opening 500 feet above the Columbia River, is between 1 and 6 miles wide, 50 miles long, and almost 1,000 feet deep.

Settling the Columbia Basin

Besides leaving the region with the spectacular coulee and other unusual land formations, the glacier left a trail of wonderful soil for crops. Fertile land and a long growing season attracted settlers in the late 1800s. Three new railroads in the area also made the land easily accessible for the first time. For several years, rainfall that was well above the area's average allowed farmers to work successful wheat farms. But eventually, the return of the region's scant rainfall resulted in widespread crop failure. As their crops died, many settlers abandoned their farms. Several individuals and organizations tried in different ways to bring water to their drought-stricken lands. Building canals, pumping water from nearby lakes, and pumping water up from deep-drilled wells all proved to be too expensive or difficult for a long-term solution.

In 1903, the government's new Reclamation Service, an agency championed by President Theodore Roosevelt, sent civil engineers to investigate ways to irrigate the area. Hopeful settlers and business people were encouraged by newspaper reports of various proposals, especially a plan known as the Big Bend Project. This plan would take water from the Pend Oreille River, a tributary of the Columbia, and deliver it to the Grand Coulee by a system of canals and tunnels. But by 1906, the government abandoned the project and other irrigation plans for the area because of the high cost.

By 1910, the number of frustrated farmers who left their land had increased. Water was needed desperately to turn 2 million acres of dry soil in the Columbia region into productive farms. In its deep canyon coursed the Columbia, the largest river in the state. The only thing missing was a practical way to harness the potentially huge resources of the river.

"If Nature Could Do It, Why Not Man?"

According to Grand Coulee legend, William M. Clapp, a local lawyer, had a new solution for the water shortage. Clapp and other area businessmen sometimes met to discuss matters of local interest. It was during one of these conversations in the summer of 1917, that Paul Donaldson, a young man pursuing mining interests in the area, described his recent work with a geologist in the coulee. Donaldson explained the geologist's theory that the coulee was carved when a glacier dammed the Columbia River, diverting its flow. Clapp seized on the idea declaring, "If nature could do it, why not man?"

President Theodore Roosevelt was a strong supporter of the Reclamation Service, which explored ways to irrigate new areas of the country.

Clapp and his friends kept their idea of a dam at the Grand Coulee private. They quietly took steps to have the board of county commissioners approve a survey of the proposed area. Norval Enger, deputy county engineer, completed the survey. He reported that the idea had potential, but the cost would be beyond what the county itself could afford. Once again, cost, the obstacle that had plagued every previous plan, seemed to be unbeatable.

The Columbia River splits off from the Pend Oreille River not far from the border between the United States and Canada.

Billy Clapp's bright idea would surely have died had it not been for the publicity it received from local newspaperman, Rufus Woods. Coverage in his *Wenatchee Daily World* of the "latest, newest, most ambitious idea in irrigation and water power" captured the imaginations of local politicians, business people, and residents.

At the same time another plan, proposed by the chairman of the State Public Service Commission, Elbert F. Blaine, also began attracting attention and support. Blaine's idea was to transport water to the Columbia basin from the Pend Oreille River in Idaho, more than 100 miles away. Because the area between the Pend Oreille River and Grand Coulee is mostly downhill, gravity would enable the water to flow through a series of canals and natural waterways to be distributed to the area's thirsty farms and grazing lands.

Public-spirited citizens, hoping to bring growth and prosperity to a region known mostly for "wheat, heat, and rattlesnakes," soon divided into two camps supporting one of the two methods of irrigation. Blaine's backers favored the "gravity plan," as his proposal soon became known. The dam's sponsors endorsed the "pumping plan," as Clapp's proposal for the dam was often called, since irrigation water would be pumped up from the reservoir formed behind the dam. Study and debate continued for 15 years before the government decided between the two plans. And it was another 15 years before water actually began to flow into the huge Columbia Basin.

River Thunder

From the beginning, the pumping plan supporters and the gravity plan supporters competed with each other. People from smaller towns in the Wenatchee/Central Washington area favored building the big dam. However, a group composed mostly of powerful businessmen from the city of Spokane and its largest employer, Washington Water Power Company, pushed for the gravity plan. Spokane officials knew a big dam producing huge amounts of electricity would reduce both their profits and their influence. On February 20, 1919, the Washington Legislature created the Columbia Basin Survey Commission and appropriated $100,000 to be used

Opposite: The Columbia is 1,243 miles long and the fourth-largest river in North America.

15

to study the rival plans. The commission, dominated by Spokane interests, issued a report favoring the gravity plan a year later. In 1921, Willis Tryon Batcheller, a Seattle engineer hired by the state, wrote a report supporting the dam and the pumping plan. Then Major General George W. Goethals, builder of the Panama Canal, was hired to make a study of the issue. His report, influenced by the Spokane interests that partly funded it, recommended the gravity plan, saying it would be simpler and cheaper to build. The political battle continued to seesaw back and forth, with the gravity plan gaining momentum.

Trading Water for Power

The climax in the struggle over the two plans came on January 21, 1927 when Congress passed the Rivers and Harbors Bill that authorized the investigation of waterways with potential power sites, including the Columbia River. From 1928–1931 the Army's Corps of Engineers, headed by Major John S. Butler, studied the river. The finished report, nearly 2,000 pages long, recommended construction of the dam and pumping irrigation water up into the Grand Coulee. The cost of irrigating Columbia basin lands would be paid for by selling the power generated by the dam.

By 1931, however, the country was hit hard by the economic disaster known as the Great Depression. A frustrated and besieged President Hoover refused to allocate funds for the dam. By the end of 1932, however, things took an upturn with the inauguration of a new president—Franklin D. Roosevelt. Roosevelt included the Grand Coulee Dam in his newly founded Public Works Administration program. In order to save money, a low dam—which would provide power but not irrigation—was approved with the possibility of adding more height to the dam later. Funds were made available to begin the Columbia Basin Project on July 27, 1933, under section 202 of the National Industrial Recovery Act. The sum of $63 million was allotted for the construction of its key structure, Grand Coulee Dam. The job of building the dam, Public Works Project #9, was assigned to the Bureau of Reclamation.

President Hoover

Several dam designs were considered, including a concrete multiple arch dam. Hoover Dam, under construction at the time, is a concrete arch dam. Finally, the design for a concrete gravity dam was chosen. In this type of structure, the huge weight of the dam is enough to keep it in place against the force of the water stored behind it. The canyon at Grand Coulee is wide and the bedrock is solid granite. Abundant materials for making concrete were nearby. A low concrete gravity dam could also serve as the foundation for construction of a high dam later.

Now someone had to build it.

A "NEW DEAL" FOR AMERICA

On Friday, October 28, 1929, disaster struck the American economy. That day, a sudden panic swept through the New York Stock Exchange on Wall Street. In the panic, investors went into a selling frenzy, drastically reducing the value of nearly every stock on the market. Hundreds of millions of dollars were lost in just a few hours. Millions of investors—wealthy on Thursday—were now nearly penniless.

That infamous October day—later known as "Black Friday"—marked the official onset of America's Great Depression. It was a time of economic hardship that would last more than 10 years. Banks failed. Businesses closed down by the score. And millions of previously hardworking citizens were suddenly unemployed, homeless, and faced with no means of survival.

Franklin Delano Roosevelt

By the time the 1932 presidential election arrived, Americans were ready for a change. During the campaign for the presidency that year, Franklin D. Roosevelt had promised the country a "New Deal," which would establish new government programs and bring the country out of the Depression. Within his first 100 days in office, Roosevelt guided 15 major new laws through Congress. One of these laws, the National Industrial Recovery Act, created the Public Works Administration (PWA). The agency was authorized to make loans to states, cities, and other public bodies for construction projects

Panic on Wall Street during the stock market crash of 1929.

that developed the nation's resources and provided jobs for millions of workers left unemployed by the Depression. Between 1933 and 1939, the PWA helped fund the construction of 70% of the country's new schools, 65% of its courthouses, city halls, and sewage plants, 35% of hospitals and other health service buildings, and 10% of all the roads, bridges, and subways built. Nearly 5 billion hours of employment were created, $6 billion spent, and 34,000 projects completed. Some PWA projects were: the Tennessee Valley Authority; The Grand Coulee, Bonneville, Hoover, and Fort Peck dams; New York City's Triboro Bridge; and Chicago's sewage system.

Hoover Dam

Bonneville Dam

3

"The Biggest Thing On Earth"

On August 1, 1933, Frank A. Banks arrived at the dam site. Banks, who had been appointed chief engineer for Grand Coulee Dam, was a 30-year veteran of dam projects.

Almost a year later, Banks presided as bids were submitted by contractors anxious to build the huge project. Three companies—Silas Mason Co., Walsh Co., and Atkinson-Kier Co.—joined under the name MWAK Co. to submit the winning bid of $29,339,301.50. In a surprise upset, MWAK beat out the favored competition—Six Companies. Six Companies, the group that was finishing Boulder (now Hoover) Dam, submitted a bid more than $5

21

million higher. On July 13, 1934, Secretary of the Interior, Harold Ickes, officially awarded the contract to MWAK Co. The contract gave MWAK four and a half years to build the second-largest dam in the world. It would be 350 feet high and 3,400 feet long, containing more than 3 million cubic yards of concrete. Only Boulder Dam was larger. With 30 days notice, the government also had the option to switch to a high dam, so Grand Coulee could be used for irrigation as well. If the high dam was built, it would make Grand Coulee larger than Boulder Dam (and thus, the largest dam in the world). On June 5, 1935, dam supporters had reason

This aerial photo shows the Grand Coulee construction site in 1935.

to celebrate. Harold Ickes signed a change order to build the high dam. Now the Columbia Basin would get both power and water.

Before work began, however, there were many challenges that still had to be met.

Transportation and Towns

No railroad passed near the dam site, and roads and bridges in the area were inadequate to transport the materials needed for the huge project. To solve this problem, 32 miles of new railroad track were laid and a new bridge spanning the river was built. More than $600,000 was also spent to construct or improve roads and bridges in the area. Workers even leveled a rough runway to serve as an airport.

Before work began, housing and services for the thousands who would build the dam did not exist in this isolated area. People lived in tents, tarpaper shacks, even cardboard boxes, hoping to grab a job. Then, the government built its engineers and foremen a tree-lined model city called "Engineer's Town." Nearby, MWAK Co. built Mason City for its workers. Billed as the world's first "all electric city," it boasted stores, churches, parks, a hotel, schools, and even a hospital. Workers with families paid between $32 and $38 a month to rent a three- or four-bedroom house. The neighboring, newly formed town of Grand Coulee had a more "wild west" atmosphere, with bars and dance halls outnumbering schools. By 1935, there were 8 towns and more than 12,000 people living within 12 miles of the dam.

Cofferdams and Timber Cribs

The costs and dangers involved in containing the thundering Columbia River were not to be taken lightly. These dangers caused most of the contractors who had hoped to submit bids for the project to abandon their plans. MWAK had successfully outbid the remaining competition because they developed a money-saving plan to divert the river. Instead of re-routing it around the job site through tunnels dug in the canyon walls, they would protect the work areas

T<small>HE</small> W<small>ORLD'S</small> L<small>ARGEST</small> C<small>ONVEYOR</small> B<small>ELTS</small>

To fully expose the granite bedrock on which Grand Coulee Dam would rest, about 12 million cubic yards of rock and earth—more than the volume of the dam itself—had to be removed. MWAK Co. pioneered the use of the world's largest conveyor belt system to transport the excavated materials away from the site. The 5-foot-wide rubber belts cost $750,000 and ultimately stretched 2 miles in length. Each day, huge electric shovels scooped up an average of 55,000 cubic yards of jumbled sand, gravel, clay, and boulders and fed the mixture onto the system. A device called a "grizzly" separated out large rocks that could damage the belts. The continuously moving "river of dirt" traveled a mile, climbed 500 feet to a canyon, and discharged its flow at the dump site there—at the rate of a ton per second! Though the belts ran with speed and efficiency, operating them

could be dangerous work. In total, four people died using them. Two accidents occurred in January of 1935, when workers were caught between the conveyor belt and the rollers on which it ran. Heart attacks claimed two additional men working with the belts. On May 1, 1937, the excavation was complete and the conveyor belts were taken apart.

Conveyor belts were also used to supply materials to build the dam's concrete foundation. Small pebbles, called aggregate, were moved on 43 belts, from the dig site to the concrete mixing plants built at the site. Two of the belts were each 1,500 feet long. Crossing the site on the "largest suspension bridge ever built for a conveyor belt," they delivered 700 tons of material each hour to the concrete mixing plant. During a two-year period, some of those belts carried 10 million cubic yards of materials.

from the river by use of a system of coffers, or temporary, dams. The coffers would keep water away from areas that were to be excavated. Grand Coulee Dam would then be built in two pieces. First, a cofferdam would keep the river away on the west side while the riverbed was excavated down to bedrock, and the foundation was poured there. After the west side foundation was completed, two more cofferdams would be built. These cross-river dams would stretch from the east side to the completed foundation of the west side, if the plan was successful, and force the river to flow over the foundation through 32-foot-wide slots left in the concrete. MWAK would then pump out the water between the two cofferdams, prepare the bedrock, and pour the rest of the concrete.

Despite temperatures dropping to 18 degrees below zero, work began on the west bank of the river on New Year's Day, 1935. Speed was important; the builders had to finish the west side cofferdam before the river's spring rise. Approximately 1,200 men worked in three shifts 24 hours a day, racing to beat the rising river. Accidents were common—more than

Excavation for the cofferdam on the west side began in 1935.

Cross-river cofferdams were built in 1936, after the west side coffers were complete (Note: Mason City, the contractor's camp, can be seen in the distance.)

150 were recorded during the month of February alone. Less than three months later, the "world's largest cellular cofferdam" was completed. The 3,000-foot-long wall enclosed 60 acres of riverbed. A cofferdam begun in September on the east side of the river protected crews as they labored there.

In February 1936, work on the cross-river cofferdams began. When completed, the dams would make the "the world's largest timber crib."

THE "ICE DAM"

Landslides continually plagued the excavation. On November 15, 1935, approximately 2 million cubic yards of materials from the hillsides above the dam tumbled into the site. Less than a week later, a second slide swept 15 men down into the excavation site. Luckily, no one was killed.

During the spring of 1936, workers at the dam site ran into a serious problem. Wet clay on the east bank of the river started slipping down into the excavation site faster than it could be removed. Workers tried several methods to stop the approach of the 200,000-cubic-yard "mud glacier."

Every effort to halt the sliding mass failed. Then a young engineer suggested a unique solution— freezing the area. A refrigeration plant was built and a huge pipeline was buried in the clay. In August 1936, icy cold salt brine was pumped through the pipe system, freezing an "ice dam" over 40 feet high, 25 feet thick, and 100 feet wide. The plan worked, and by the end of September excavation in the area could continue. The solution cost $30,000 but it saved about $100,000 in additional excavation costs. The ice dam stayed in place for about a year.

Approximately 3 million feet of timber were used to build individual "cribs," or containers, which were then floated onto the river. Barges guided them, and divers braved the icy waters to check their position. Then the cribs were filled with gravel and faced with steel-sheet pilings. Stretching from the east bank to the completed west side of the dam, it was time to accomplish what many had declared impossible—to move the Columbia River out of its ancient bed.

But the river didn't give up without a fight. In March of 1937, water burst through the downstream cofferdam, threatening the site. Crews built a "dike" of mattresses, tumbleweeds, cable, and sacks of cement to stop the invading river. A line of trucks, stretching a mile long, dumped loads of whatever they could scrounge into the river every 10 seconds.

Skilled divers were needed throughout the construction to check on the dam's progress below the icy water.

These efforts temporarily stopped the river from invading the work site. In May, MWAK finally drove steel-sheet pilings into the riverbed to fortify the dam. This managed to solve the problem completely.

MWAK Pours the Foundation

Within the cofferdam walls, men and machines blasted and dug down to expose the bedrock in the riverbed. Engineers descended into the bedrock to inspect it through tunnels dug 3 feet wide and 30 to 200 feet deep. Cracks and seams were filled with grout to form a solid granite "dam" below to support the concrete one being built above.

On December 6, 1935, Washington's Governor Clarence Martin poured the first "official" bucket of concrete. He received a check for 75 cents, an hour's pay as a concrete worker. Although Grand Coulee Dam is now a solid mass of concrete, it was constructed as a series of more than 20,000 interlocking concrete columns. The concrete was poured to build

On December 6, 1935, the first official bucket of concrete was poured by Washington's Governor Clarence Martin.

the columns up 5 feet at a time, with 72-hour intervals between pours. Because concrete produces heat as it sets, the dam's engineers estimated it would take several hundred years for the concrete to cool.

Workers place a frame on one of the huge racks constructed to prevent trash from entering the dam's outlet system.

To solve this problem, about 1,700 miles of pipeline was embedded in the concrete as it was poured. River water was pumped through the pipes to cool the concrete and prevent cracking. By August 1936, a million yards of concrete had been placed in the dam. A year later, workers laid 15,844 cubic yards of concrete in a single day, a new world record.

On January 10, 1938, MWAK completed its contract. The company had placed 4,525,209 cubic yards of concrete and had employed about 11,000 workers. It had cost nearly $40 million and the lives of 60 people to build the great dam's foundation.

The High Dam

With the dam's foundation complete, the government was ready to accept bids to complete the monumental high dam. Realizing that the project was too big and expensive for any single company to manage, former rivals MWAK and Six Companies united to form Interior Construction (later re-named Consolidated Builders, Inc. or CBI) and submitted the winning bid of $34,442,240. CBI, made up of 10 of the country's largest construction companies—would build what was then called "the biggest thing on earth."

The first concrete for the high dam was poured on July 23, 1938. The construction followed the same basic routine as MWAK's low dam, but with reduced time between pours. Nearly 200 feet above the foundation, 7 huge cranes traveled along a 3,600-foot-long tressel that stretched across the river. They delivered concrete and other materials to all parts of the dam. Massive portable gates dispersed the river through slots left in the foundation.

By June 1941, the dam was nearly complete and already generating hydroelectric power.

In 1939, the project surpassed a number of records and firsts. Three shifts of 2,000 men each worked around the clock daily. On May 25, 1939, crews set a world record when they poured 20,685 cubic yards of concrete in a 24-hour period. During 1939, a total of 3,650,000 cubic yards of concrete were poured, four times the amount poured in 1938. By the end of 1939, the shell of the west powerhouse building was already completed. Excavation and pouring of the first concrete for the pumping plant was now begun. The pumping plant would actually bring water—and thus, irrigation—to the area.

Though the rapid progress was impressive, the price of speed was high. In the first year, a total of 18 people died—most from falls and falling equipment. Nearly 500 accidents were reported during this second phase of the dam's construction. Despite the rumors, no one was buried in the concrete. CBI took over the hospital in Mason City and created a guaranteed medical plan for its employees. The plan, named for CBI's president, Henry Kaiser, was the beginning of Kaiser Permanente Medical Care Program, which is still in operation today.

With the threat of WWII looming, construction continued to proceed rapidly. In1941, two years ahead of schedule, power began generating at Grand Coulee Dam. On December 12, 1941, CBI completed concrete placement at the dam. Just 23 years after Billy Clapp's "bright idea" had appeared in Rufus Woods' newspaper, Grand Coulee Dam stood above the great river. Only small jobs and clean-up remained for the following year. On January 1, 1943, the Bureau of Reclamation officially took over operation of the dam.

It had cost the government $162,610,943 to build Grand Coulee Dam. Construction workers, engineers, farmers, lawyers, business people, politicians, and presidents had all worked together to accomplish it. The huge dam was a fitting monument to their efforts.

4

"Roll On, Columbia, Roll On"

Ceremonies marking the start of power production—two years ahead of schedule—took place on March 22, 1941. On October 4, 1941, the world's first 108,000 kilowatt generator went into service at the dam. As World War II erupted, five more generators were quickly completed and installed. To aid the war effort, two smaller units, which were scheduled to be placed in Shasta Dam in California, were also temporarily installed in Grand Coulee Dam.

Opposite: When the dam was officially dedicated in 1950, there was still much work that had not been finished.

35

The Power of a Million Horses

The tremendous power output from Grand Coulee was channeled into the production of warships, warplanes, and ammunition. It is estimated that one-third of the planes built during World War II were manufactured from aluminum produced with Grand Coulee electric power. The secret Hanford atomic bomb project, also powered by Grand Coulee Dam, was another major factor in ending the war.

When President Harry S. Truman dedicated Grand Coulee Dam on May 11, 1950, neither the powerplant nor the irrigation works were complete. There was still work to be done, and soon a new chapter in the dam's history would be written with the addition of a third powerhouse. Even today, more than 90 years since Billy Clapp's bright idea, the story of Grand Coulee Dam remains unfinished. Parts of the irrigation works and the third powerhouse are still incomplete.

President Harry S. Truman waits for the signal before pressing a button that would officially "start up" the Grand Coulee Dam.

THE THIRD POWERHOUSE

After World War II, the Pacific Northwest's continuing boom in development caused it to experience frequent power shortages. To solve this problem, the Bureau of Reclamation proposed construction of a third powerhouse at Grand Coulee Dam. On June 14, 1966, President Lyndon Johnson signed a bill appropriating funds to begin construction, and work began in 1967. The plans called for a 260-foot section of the original dam to be blasted, clearing the way for a 1,170 foot forebay dam to be joined at an angle. Four companies joined to submit the winning bid of $112,525,612—the largest contract ever awarded by the Bureau of Reclamation. On October 21, 1970, the first official load of concrete was poured; workers threw pennies onto the bedrock symbolically cementing their contribution to the dam. It took eight years—approximately the same amount of time it took to build the dam—for the third powerhouse building to be constructed. More than 2,000 workers labored at the site. Women, who were barred from construction on the original dam, were hired in 1970, including the Bureau of Reclamation's first female civil engineer on a heavy construction job, Toby Ann Levy. By 1975, the building was complete. The last of six generators was put into place in the spring of 1980, making Grand Coulee Dam the world's largest power generating station. On July 16, 1983, nearly 50 years after the symbolic first stake was driven signaling the start of the Grand Coulee Dam's construction, the third powerhouse was dedicated. At 20 stories high, it spread over an area equal to 4 city blocks. The American Society of Civil Engineers cited the third powerhouse as the country's outstanding engineering achievement of that year.

In 1951, approximately 18 years after the beginning of the dam's construction, the powerplant was completed as originally planned. The largest powerplant in the Western Hemisphere at the time, each of its two powerhouses stood as tall as a 13-story building. Eighteen generators, each weighing about 1,000 tons, occupied the twin generating rooms. These rooms were each twice as large as a baseball stadium. Today, the record-breaking equipment and facilities of earlier times are dwarfed by the massive third powerhouse.

Franklin D. Roosevelt Lake

In 1937, crews began clearing part of the 80,000 soon-to-be flooded acres that would become the reservoir behind the Grand Coulee Dam. It became the largest undertaking accomplished by the Work Projects Administration (WPA). The job required the efforts of more than 2,000 men working out of 7 camps along the river. Others worked in remote spots on the dam's upper reaches from floating bunkhouses built on barges that the workers called Camp Ferry. Thousands of acres of trees were felled. And more than 2,000 homes and buildings, miles of roads and railroad tracks, and 3 cemeteries were removed or relocated. Water would eventually cover nearly a dozen towns.

On June 1, 1942, about 15,000 people gathered to witness the first water from the nearly full

At the official dedication ceremony, fifty women—representing the fifty states—each pour the first water into the reservoir that was connected to Franklin D. Roosevelt Lake.

NATIVE AMERICAN TRADITIONS LOST

When the government began acquiring land in the area that would later become Franklin D. Roosevelt Lake, it encountered problems with two Native American tribes, the Colville and the Spokane. Both tribes lived on reservations, part of which were within the reservoir boundaries. Several issues made the discussion of payment for these lands complicated. First, for centuries the tribes had buried their dead in the area. Although more than 1,200 graves were eventually discovered and relocated, thousands were lost. Second, these Native Americans had come for centuries to fish for the salmon that came to the river each spring. Treaties had guaranteed the tribes' rights to fish at Kettle Falls forever. But as the waters rose behind the dam drowning the area, representatives from tribes throughout the Pacific Northwest gathered on the river banks for a Ceremony of Tears. The govern-

ment made fairly successful efforts to build fish hatcheries and relocate the salmon to other tributaries of the river. But an important part of the tribes' livelihood and a traditional way of life was destroyed forever.

In 1951, the dispute was argued in court. The Colville Confederated Tribes and the Spokane Tribes filed a claim against the government. In 1975 they claimed $100 million in damages and demanded a share of the profits from the power generated by the dam. In a film called *The Price We Paid*, they detailed the loss of their lands, their ancestral burying grounds, and their way of life. Talks dragged on for almost 20 years. Finally, in March of 1994, the government agreed to pay a lump sum of $53 million dollars. A minimum of $15.25 million, representing the tribes' share of the power profits, would also be paid to them annually.

reservoir trickle, then deluge, down the spillway, creating a waterfall twice as high as Niagara Falls.

As part of the dedication ceremonies for the dam in 1950, the reservoir was named Franklin D. Roosevelt Lake, in honor of the 32nd president who championed the dam's construction. Today, Franklin D. Roosevelt Lake is the largest lake in Washington, stretching 151 miles, all the way to the border between the United States and Canada with approximately 660 miles of shoreline. When full, it covers 130 square miles and contains more than 9.5 million acre feet of water. The lake is a federally owned reservoir operated by the Bureau of Reclamation. Recreation on the lake—fishing, boating, hunting, and water sports—is managed cooperatively by three government agencies and two Native American tribes, the Colville and the Spokane.

The reservoir is also used for flood control measures each spring, as the water level is lowered to make space for spring and summer runoff from melting snow in the Rocky Mountains.

The Promised Land

The dream of irrigated land surrounding the Columbia River that inspired construction of Grand Coulee Dam was realized in 1952. The first water from its reservoir was delivered to a farm built and planted in a single day by the Bureau of Reclamation to mark the occasion. Today, water supplied by Grand Coulee Dam irrigates more than 500,000 acres of farmland. This area, approximately twice the size of the state of Delaware, is only half of the proposed acreage originally planned. Water from Lake Roosevelt is lifted 280 feet up a hillside by 12 pumps into the Banks Lake Reservoir. Each of the machines can pump more than 780,000 gallons per minute and can supply a city the size of Chicago with its water needs. From the reservoir, water is supplied to the area through miles of

One of the Grand Coulee's canals, under construction. From the reservoirs at Grand Coulee, canals, tunnels, and waterways bring water to dry and remote areas.

canals, tunnels, and other waterways. Irrigated lands produce grains, beans, fruits, sugar beets, sweet corn, and potatoes. Dairy cows and beef cattle also graze on irrigated acres.

The control room at Grand Coulee houses computers and monitoring systems for all the dam's major functions.

Grand Coulee's Grand Show

In 1976, the government built a $1.5 million visitor center. Today, summer visitors to Grand Coulee Dam can learn its dramatic history during a spectacular laser-light show, authorized by Congress to enhance visitors' appreciation of this enormous federal project. Four lasers beam 300-foot-high images across sheets of white water spilling down the face of the dam. The river's thunder provides the soundtrack to the giant dam's story—a tribute to the determination of the thousands of Americans who contributed to its creation.

The dam serves as the backdrop for an impressive
nighttime laser light show. Although it is nearly
60 years old, the Grand Coulee Dam remains the
single greatest source of hydroelectric power in the
United States.

GLOSSARY

Cofferdam a watertight enclosure from which water is pumped to expose the bottom of a body of water for construction.

Coulee a dry riverbed.

Dike a high wall or dam that is used to hold back water or prevent flooding.

Drought a long period of dry weather.

Fertile condition that is good for growing crops.

Geologist a scientist who studies the layers of Earth's rocks and soil.

Inadequate not enough, or not good enough.

Inauguration a cermony in which a public official is sworn into office.

Irrigation to supply water for crops by artificial means, such as channels and pipes.

Plateau an area of high, flat land.

Reservation an area of land that is set aside by government for special purposes. Many Native Americans were forced onto them when settlers took over their land.

Survey to study and measure an area to make a map or a plan.

Treaties formal agreements between two parties.

Tressel a framework that supports a bridge or railroad track.

Tributary a smaller river or stream that runs into a larger river or stream.

CHRONOLOGY

1919 Columbia Basin Survey Commission funds studies of ways to irrigate Columbia Basin.

1927 Passage of Rivers and Harbors Bill authorizes Army Corps of Engineers to study rivers, including Columbia, with potential power sites.

1932 Army Corps of Engineers study recommends construction of high dam at Grand Coulee.

1933 National Industrial Recovery Act passes Congress and authorizes the funding and construction of the Columbia Basin Project and Grand Coulee Dam. Excavation of dam site begins.

1934 MWAK Company bids on and wins contract to build low dam at Grand Coulee.

1935 Work begins on Columbia River diversion.
Secretary of the Interior Harold Ickes signs change order authorizing high dam construction at Grand Coulee.
First concrete poured in base of dam in December.

1937 Reservoir begins to fill behind dam construction.

1938 MWAK completes the dam's foundation.
Consolidated Builders, Inc. is awarded the contract to complete the high dam.
First concrete is poured for high dam.

1941 First power generated by Grand Coulee Dam power plant. Last concrete placed in dam on December 12.

1942 Franklin D. Roosevelt Lake is filled.

1943 Bureau of Reclamation takes over dam's operation.

1950 President Truman dedicates Grand Coulee Dam.

1952 First irrigation water delivered by pumping plant.

1970 First concrete is poured for third powerhouse.

1976 New $1.5 million dollar Visitor Center opens.

1983 Third powerhouse is dedicated.
American Society of Civil Engineers cites third powerhouse as the Outstanding Engineering Achievement of 1983.

1994 Federal government agrees to pay Colville Confederated Tribes $53 million compensating them for the loss of tribal lands, burial sites, and salmon fishing due to the dam's construction.

For More Information

Books

Brown, Warren. Russell Train. *Alternative Sources of Energy* (Earth at Risk). New York, NY: Chelsea House, 1993.

Doherty, Craig. Katherine Doherty. *Hoover Dam* (Building America). Woodbridge, CT: Blackbirch Press, Inc., 1995.

Dunn, Andrew. *Dams.* New York, NY: Thomson Learning, 1993.

Maze, Stephanie. Catherine Grace (Contributor). Peter Menzel (Illustrator). *I Want to be an Engineer* (I Want to be). Orlando, FL: Harcourt Brace, 1997.

Video

Arts & Entertainment Home Video. *Grand Coulee Dam* (Modern Marvels), 1994.

Web Sites

Columbia Basin Project

Find out about hydroelectric power generation, view the photo gallery, and read more about the history of the dam— users.owt.com/chubbard/gcdam/index.html

Grand Coulee Dam

Learn more about the statistics, functions, and design of the dam— borworld.usbr.gov/cdams/dams/grandcoulee.html

Source Notes

Downs, L. Vaughn. *The Mightiest of the All: Memories of Grand Coulee Dam.* New York: ASCE Press, 1993.

Morgan, Murray. *The Dam.* New York: Viking Press, 1954.

Pitzer, Paul C. *Grand Coulee Dam: Harnessing a Dream.* Pullman, Washington: Washington State University Press, 1994.

Sundborg, George. *Hail Columbia: The Thirty Year Struggle for Grand Coulee Dam*. New York, Macmillan, 1954.

The Story of the Columbia Basin Project. Washington, D.C.: U.S. Department of the Interior, Government Printing Office, 1964.

"Columbia Basin Project." Pacific Northwest Region: Bureau of Reclamation, Project Data Book, 1983.

"Columbia Basin Project." United States Department of the Interior, Government Printing Office, 1950.

"Modern Marvels: Grand Coulee Dam. A & E Networks, 1994.

INDEX